PHOTOGRAPHS OF
GLASGOW

COLIN BAXTER

GLASGOW

'Dear Green Place', 'Second City of the Empire', 'Glesga'; Scotland's largest city has had many historic incarnations since in the 6th century St Mungo founded a settlement on the banks of the River Clyde.

At the start of the 18th century the population of Glasgow was only 12,000, but by the end of the 19th century it had topped the one million mark. Trade in tobacco, sugar and cotton combined with the deepening of the Clyde brought wealth and prosperity. The Industrial Revolution saw the city as a world leader in steel production and shipbuilding, becoming the workshop of the British Empire. Glasgow was transformed and expanded westwards along the Clyde to accommodate the aspirations of its merchants, city elders and the thousands from the Lowlands, the Highlands, Ireland and beyond, who worked in the factories and shipyards, and who made Glasgow their home.

The late 20th century then saw the inexorable decline of heavy industry and Glasgow faced the considerable challenges of an uncertain future, before re-emerging as the vibrant and dynamic city it is today. An industrial past has been succeeded by a commercial and cultural present.

A bustling and cosmopolitan centre takes you up Sauchiehall Street, doon Buchanan Street and alang Argyle where modernity intermingles with Victorian architecture. The West End surrounds Glasgow's other river, the Kelvin, with tenements jostling amenably with the facades of the University of Glasgow and Kelvingrove Museum and Art Gallery. Whilst a leafy South Side boasts not only the peace and quiet of Pollock Country Park, but also the roar and passion of Scotland's national stadium, Hampden Park.

Above all though, Glasgow is a city of the people. Friendly, industrious and gallus folk, that from the days of St Mungo have built the homes, museums, stadiums and parks and have made Glasgow a city reknowned throughout the world, a 'dear green place' that one would be proud to belong to.

THE CITY CHAMBERS, GEORGE SQUARE – When inaugurated by Queen Victoria in 1888 the City Chambers became the imposing civic centrepiece of 19th century Glasgow. It has been the headquarters of the reconstituted Glasgow City Council since 1996.

COAT OF ARMS, CITY CENTRE – The story of Glasgow began with a small fishing settlement on the banks of the River Clyde that in the 6th century saw the foundation of a monastery by St Mungo. Glasgow's Coat of Arms reflects this history and features the tree, the bird, the fish and the bell – all symbols associated with the life of Glasgow's patron saint.

THE RIVER CLYDE – looking east towards the city centre.

THE CITY CENTRE from the air (opposite) – Glasgow boasts a modern, vibrant and bustling centre in keeping with being the largest city in Scotland. GLASGOW FOLK (above) in all their many shapes and guises, off to work, to shop, socialise and generally going about their business.

THE RIVER CLYDE, CITY CENTRE – Glasgow expanded as a port and major trading centre on both banks of the River Clyde. Goods and produce flooded into the city, enabling commerce to flourish and shopkeepers throughout Glasgow to give their customers a taste of near and far.

PARTICK.   CANDLERIGGS.

HUTCHESONS HALL, MERCHANT CITY.　　　BLACKFRIARS STREET, MERCHANT CITY.

THE ITALIAN CENTRE, MERCHANT CITY.

The world's last working paddle steamer, *PS WAVERLEY*, on the River Clyde.

BOTANIC GARDENS, WEST END – created in 1817 in Kelvinside and a welcome oasis of tranquillity away from the hurly-burly of the West End. The centrepieces of the Gardens are its impressive glasshouses and tropical plant collection in the Victorian built Kibble Palace.

TOLBOOTH, GLASGOW CROSS (right) –
The seven storeys high Tolbooth Steeple
is the only remaining part of the
Tolbooth, one of the most important
buildings in Glasgow's history, where
resided the Town Clerk, the council and
the city's prison. Strategically situated
at the junction of five streets, all roads
led to Glasgow Cross.

MERCHANT CITY (left) – The Merchant
City in Glasgow's city centre has a long
and varied history. Recent redevelopment
has transformed it into a prestigious
residential, commercial and cultural
district and seen the area hark back
to its illustrious past, when the wealthy
merchants and 'tobacco lords' of the 18th
century began building residences in
keeping with their new-found prosperity.

BAIRD HALL, SAUCHIEHALL STREET (left)
– Originally built as the Beresford Hotel
in 1938, the Baird Hall's modern art-deco
design caused considerable comment
at the time, but has since become one
of the best-known examples of 1930s
architecture in Glasgow.

TRADESTON BRIDGE, CITY CENTRE
(right) – known to one and all as
the 'SQUIGGLY BRIDGE' because of
its innovative winding S-shape.
The Tradeston Bridge was opened to
pedestrians and cyclists in 2009 and
links Tradeston on the south side of the
River Clyde to Broomielaw to the north,
becoming a symbol of regeneration
along the waterfront.

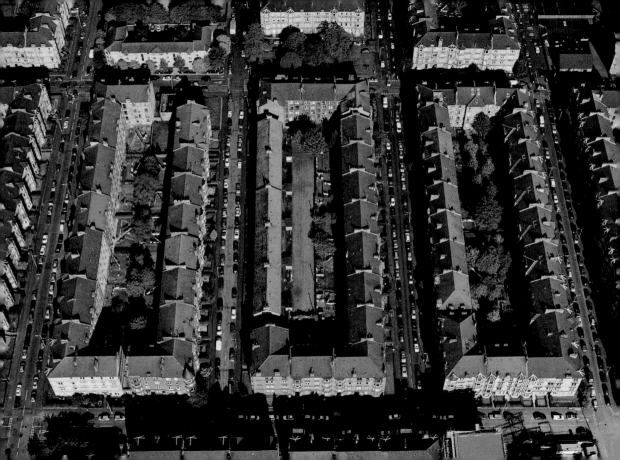

DENNISTOUN TENEMENTS (left) and HILLHEAD DOORWAYS (above).

CITY CHAMBERS, GEORGE SQUARE.

ARGYLE STREET – in a blizzard!

ST GEORGE'S MANSION'S & WEST END SPIRES.

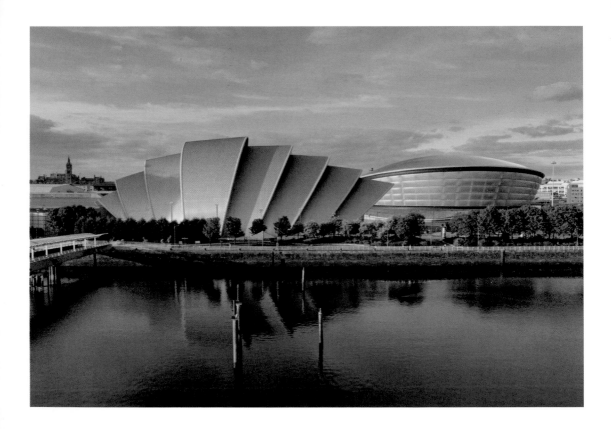

GLASGOW COAT OF ARMS,
CATHEDRAL SQUARE (right) –
Another example on this old gas lamp
of the Glasgow coat of arms, inspired
by St Mungo. The coat of arms in
a variety of designs, can be found
throughout the city, with the tree,
the bird, the fish and the bell
all represented.

THE CLYDE AUDITORIUM and 'THE HYDRO'
(left) – Alongside the River Clyde adjacent
to the Scottish Exhibition and Conference
Centre, the Clyde Auditorium was opened
in 1997. It is affectionately known as
'THE ARMADILLO' due to its unique design
and has become an iconic landmark in
modern Glasgow, even though the original
inspiration for the building was a ship's
hull. The futuristic structure to the right
is 'The SSE Hydro'. It was opened in 2013
and is one of the busiest multi-purpose
indoor arenas in the world.

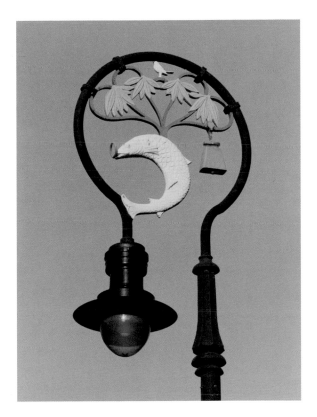

THE UNIVERSITY OF GLASGOW
(left, and right from the air) – Founded
in 1451 as Scotland's second university
and moving to its current home on
Gilmorehill in the West End in 1870,
the University of Glasgow overlooks
Kelvingrove Park and the equally
imposing Museum and Art Gallery.
Many national and international
figures have studied and taught here
through a long and illustrious history,
with perhaps appropriately the
most distinguished being renowned
physicist Lord Kelvin.

GLASGOW GREEN & THE RIVER CLYDE (opposite) – Glasgow Green is the oldest public park in the city dating back over 500 years. The PEOPLE'S PALACE & WINTER GARDENS, Glasgow Green (above) – was opened in 1898 as a cultural centre. Today it serves as Glasgow's social history museum.

CENTRAL STATION – above Argyle Street, City Centre.

HOPE STREET, CITY CENTRE.

WEST GEORGE STREET, CITY CENTRE.

TILES IN CLOSES, SOUTH SIDE.

WEST END WINDOW – Intricate designs and motifs are examples of the 'Glasgow style' and can be found throughout the city in settings both large and small.

CARDONALD – in the southwest of the city. Cardonald was first developed in the 1920s as a residential suburb and was the location of Glasgow's first ever high-rise flats.

PRINCES SQUARE, Buchanan Street, City Centre – Originally built in 1842, Princes Square was refurbished and reopened in 1987 as the ultimate six-floor shopping centre experience and unabashedly upmarket. The decoration above the entrance (above) and the interior (right).

FINNIESTON QUAY CRANE – The 165 feet (50 metres) tall crane on the north bank of the River Clyde has not been used for its original purpose of lifting heavy machinery onto ships since the 1990s, but has become an important symbol of Glasgow's engineering past. The industry may have long gone, but Finnieston Crane remains as an immortal Glasgow landmark.

GALLERY OF MODERN ART.

UNIVERSITY OF GLASGOW.

OLD GAS LAMPOST.

WEST END.

THE DOGE'S PALACE, GLASGOW GREEN.

GEORGE SQUARE (right) – the principal square in Glasgow since 1781. George Square was named in honour of King George III and is the location for many memorials and statues of prominent historical figures and notable Glaswegians. George Square's benign and tranquil appearance belies an history of public concerts and demonstrations. The most famous was the 1919 'Black Friday' rally when 90,000 people crowded into the square to campaign for improved working conditions in the city's factories.

CLYDE ARC, popularly known as 'THE SQUINTY BRIDGE' – Completed in 2006, the road bridge connects Finnieston on the north bank of the River Clyde with Pacific Quay to the south, allowing greatly improved access to the Glasgow Science Centre complex.

GLASGOW SCHOOL OF ART –
Completed in 1899 on Garnethill
above Sauchiehall Street, Glasgow
School of Art is renowned as the
masterwork of design genius Charles
Rennie Mackintosh. Now recognised
as one of Glasgow's favourite sons,
in his lifetime Mackintosh's unique
vision was considered too radical and
modern for most. Today the building
remains in full use as the centrepiece
of Glasgow School of Art, as well
as being open to visitors. The West
Face (far left), the East Face (left)
and the North Face and Front
Entrance (right).

GLASGOW SCIENCE CENTRE (left) – opened in 2001 at Pacific Quay on the south bank of the River Clyde. The Glasgow Science Centre has become one of Glasgow's most popular visitor attractions and continues the city's long tradition for scientific and technological innovation.

GEORGE STREET, CITY CENTRE (right) – Heading east and west from George Square and the City Chambers in the city centre, George Street, along with St Vincent Street running parallel, represent modern Glasgow's ability to combine and contrast modern functionality with its Victorian architectural heritage.

POLLOCK HOUSE, Pollock Country Park – on the South Side of the city.

THE BURRELL COLLECTION, Pollock Country Park – Opened in 1983 and named after millionaire Glasgow ship-owner and philanthropist William Burrell, the building is home to the vast art collection that Burrell had acquired and then gifted to his native city.

KELVINGROVE ART GALLERY & MUSEUM – opened in 1901 as the Palace of Fine Arts for the Glasgow International Exhibition held that year. The museum was built using Dumfriesshire red sandstone and is the most popular free-to-enter visitor attraction in all of Scotland.

CHARING CROSS MANSIONS.

WILLOW TEA ROOMS, Sauchiehall Street (above) – designed by Charles Rennie Mackintosh along with the HOUSE FOR AN ART LOVER (opposite) in Bellahouston Park, the plans for which were drawn by Mackintosh in 1901 with construction belatedly taking place between 1989 and 1996.

THE GROSVENOR BUILDING, GORDON STREET, City Centre (right) – Built in 1859, the Grosvenor Building was a landmark city centre project by another visionary architect based in Glasgow, Alexander 'Greek' Thomson. As with Mackintosh, Thomson was long overlooked both at home and abroad, but has in recent years become internationally acclaimed.

FINNIESTON QUAY and the RIVER CLYDE (opposite) – Looking west along the north bank of the River Clyde, the mighty Finnieston Crane in the foreground dwarfs even its neighbours, the Clyde Auditorium, better known as 'The Armadillo', and 'The Hydro' indoor arena, symbolic structures of both past and present eras on the Clyde.

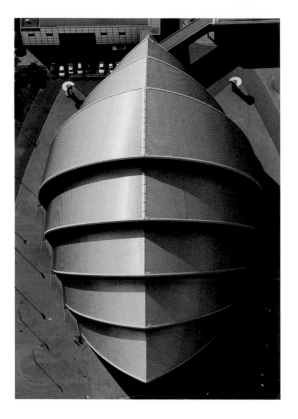

THE CLYDE AUDITORIUM (left) –
When you see the Clyde Auditorium
from above one can fully appreciate
its armour plated appearance and
how appropriate the nickname
of 'The Armadillo' truly is.

GLASGOW TOWER, GLASGOW SCIENCE
CENTRE and IMAX THEATRE (right) –
Stretching out on reclaimed land into
the River Clyde the Glasgow Science Centre
complex looks suitably futuristic from the
air. At 417 feet (127 metres) the Glasgow
Tower is the tallest tower in Scotland and
can actually rotate through 360 degrees.

TENEMENTS, GREAT WESTERN ROAD (right) – Completed in the 1840s and connecting the city centre to the West End, Great Western Road is Glasgow's longest and straightest road at over three miles long. As the city expanded westwards, tenements were built to house the many folk and Great Western Road remains predominantly residential to this day.

POLLOCKSHIELDS (left) – Developed in the 19th century as a desirable Victorian residential area on Glasgow's South Side, the district of Pollockshields has made great efforts to conserve its original vision and remains a leafy suburb close to the heart of the city.

GLASGOW CATHEDRAL –
Built in the 13th century on the
site where St Mungo (or as he is also
know St Kentigern) was said to have
built his original church centuries
before, the magnificent gothic
Glasgow Cathedral is also known
as St Mungo's or St Kentigern's in
honour of the city's patron saint.
Glasgow Cathedral is unique amongst
medieval Scottish cathedrals, in that
it survived the Reformation relatively
intact and remains as impressive
today as when it was first
constructed.

GLASGOW AT DUSK – A city known for its vibrant nightlife.
A characteristicly warm and different side of Glasgow reveals itself at dusk.
KELVINGROVE ART GALLERY & MUSEUM (opposite) and MEADOWSIDE QUAY (above).

'LET GLASGOW FLOURISH' – A proud people, an illustrious history and a richly diverse city.
THE CITY CHAMBERS, GEORGE SQUARE (above) with PARK CIRCUS and PARK QUADRANT,
KELVINGROVE (opposite). The city of Glasgow more than lives up to its motto.

TRADESTONE BRIDGE – 'The Squiggly Bridge' and the River Clyde, City Centre.

Published in Great Britain in 2011 by Colin Baxter Photography Ltd,
Grantown-on-Spey, Moray PH26 3TA, Scotland

www.colinbaxter.co.uk
Revised edition 2017

Photographs © Colin Baxter 2017   Text by John E. Abernethy
Copyright © Colin Baxter Photography Ltd 2017   All rights reserved.

A CIP Catalogue record for this book is available
from the British Library.

ISBN 978-1-84107-165-7   Printed in China

Front cover photograph: 'THE SQUINTY BRIDGE' & the River Clyde.
Back cover photograph: TENEMENTS, HIGH STREET.

Page one photograph: CHARLES RENNIE MACKINTOSH –
Glass Panel detail in the Hunterian Art Gallery, University of Glasgow.
Page two photograph: KELVINGROVE ART GALLERY & MUSEUM.